SUBMARINES

by Matt Doeden

Lerner Publications Company • Minneapolis

Lerner Publications Company
A division of Lerner Publishing Group
241 First Avenue North
Minneapolis, MN 55401 USA

Website address: www.lernerbooks.com

Words in **bold type** are explained in a glossary on page 30.

Library of Congress Cataloging-in-Publication Data

Doeden, Matt.
    Submarines / by Matt Doeden.
      p. cm. — (Pull ahead books)
    Includes index.
    ISBN-13: 978-0-8225-2669-8 (lib. bdg. : alk. paper)
    ISBN-10: 0-8225-2669-7 (lib. bdg. : alk. paper)
    1. Submarines (Ships)—Juvenile literature. I. Title.
  II. Series.
  V857.D64 2006
  623.825'7—dc22   2005001204

Manufactured in the United States of America
1 2 3 4 5 6 — JR — 11 10 09 08 07 06

Look! What is coming out of
the ocean?

It is a submarine. Submarines travel all around the world.

Submarines are ships that go underwater. They can go very deep.

Submarines can stay underwater for a
very long time. What do submarines
do underwater?

Some submarines are used to explore the ocean.

Many submarines are used for fighting. They look for ships and other submarines.

Most submarines used for fighting
carry **torpedoes**.

Submarines fire torpedoes at other ships.
Torpedoes are fired from torpedo tubes.
Sailors make sure torpedo tubes are
ready to fire.

Who is in
charge of a
submarine?

The captain is in charge of a submarine.
The captain tells the other sailors what
to do.

There are many jobs to do on
a submarine.

Sailors keep the engine running.
They clean the engine and fix parts
that break.

Sailors on submarines work hard. They
need good food to eat. The room
where sailors eat is called the **mess**.

Sailors use a submarine's radio to call sailors on other ships.

the water
marine is

The ocean is very dark. How do
sailors on submarines see what is
going on underwater?

17

Sailors use **sonar** to find their w
underwater. Sonar uses sound
guide submarines.

Periscopes can rise above
even when most of the sub
still underwater.

What makes submarines move through the water?

Submarines have huge engines.

Engines turn **propellers** on submarines.
Spinning propellers push submarines
through the water.

Sailors steer a submarine by turning a wheel. The wheel is attached to a submarine's **rudder**.

How do submarines sink and float?

Submarines carry large empty tanks.
Sailors fill the tanks with water to sink
submarines. They fill the tanks with air
when they want submarines to float.

Submarines sail all around the world. You never know where one will pop up next!

Facts about Submarines

- The first submarine was built in 1620. It could only go about 15 feet (4.6 meters) underwater.

- The Japanese submarine *Kaiko* set a record in 1995. It dove about seven miles (11.3 kilometers) underwater. No submarine had ever gone that deep before.

- The biggest submarines in the U.S. Navy are about 560 feet (171 meters) long. That's almost as long as two football fields!

- Large submarines can carry about 150 sailors.

- Sailors on submarines are called submariners.

Parts of a Submarine

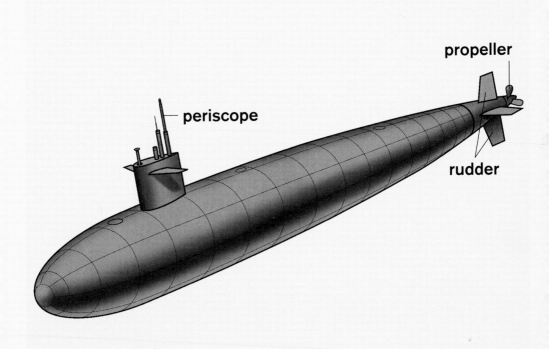

propeller

periscope

rudder

Glossary

mess: the room on a submarine where sailors eat

periscopes: long tubes that let sailors see what is happening above the water

propellers: spinning blades that push submarines through the water

rudder: the part used to steer a submarine. Sailors control the rudder from inside a submarine.

sonar: a tool sailors use to guide a submarine underwater. Sonar uses sound to make a picture of the ocean on a computer.

torpedoes: weapons that submarines carry

Index

About the Author

Matt Doeden is a freelance author and editor living in Minnesota. He has written and edited hundreds of children's books, including more than a dozen military titles.

Photo Acknowledgments

The photographs in this book appear with the permission of: U.S.Navy photos provided by Navy Visual News Service, Washington, D.C., pp. 3, 4, 5, 6, 8, 10, 11, 12, 13, 15, 16, 17,18, 19, 20, 21, 23, 24, 25, 26, 27, 31; © Stuart Westmorland/CORBIS, p.7; Steve Kaufman/CORBIS, p.9; © Yogi, Inc./CORBIS, pp.14, 22; © Laura Westlund/Interface Graphics, Inc., p.29. Front cover: U.S.Navy photos provided by Navy Visual News Service.